03 YELLOW • **BOOK 16** /air/

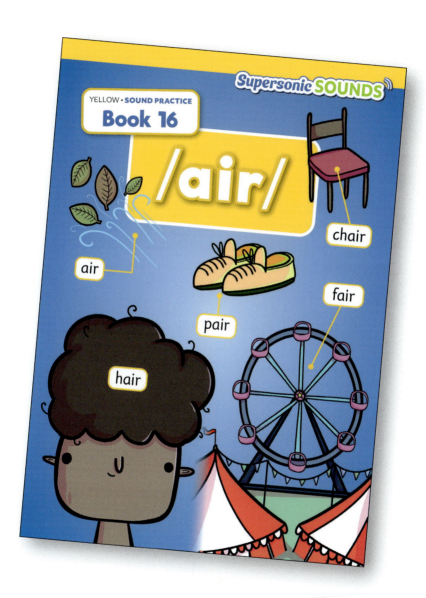

Minneapolis, Minnesota

Teaching Tips

This book focuses on the phoneme **/air/**.

Getting Started
- Review the focus phoneme of the book with readers.
- Model the sound and have readers practice themselves.

Using the Book
- Ask readers to read the words on the pages with the colorful borders, using the focus sound as their guide.
- Turn the page and check the illustration next to the word to confirm accuracy.
- As you read new words, review the word bank on the left-hand pages of the book.

Reviewing
- Encourage readers to independently reread all of the words on pages 22–23.
- Have them complete the activity on page 24 for continued practice with the focus phoneme.
- Extend the learning by asking readers if they know any other words containing the focus phoneme.

© 2025 Booklife Publishing
This edition is published by arrangement with Booklife Publishing.

North American adaptations © 2025 Bearport Publishing Company. All rights reserved. No part of this publication may be reproduced in whole or in part, stored in any retrieval system, or transmitted in any form or by any means, electronic, mechanical, photocopying, recording, or otherwise, without written permission from the publisher. Bearport Publishing is a division of Chrysalis Education Group.

For more information, write to Bearport Publishing, 5357 Penn Avenue South, Minneapolis, MN 55419.

air

air

air
chair

chair

chair

air

chair

fair

fair

fair

air
chair
fair
hair

hair

hair

air
chair
fair
hair
pair

pair

pair

air

chair

hair

fair

pair

Say the sound and trace the letters with your finger.